Straightforward Guides

A Straightforward Guide
To

FREELANCE WRITING

STEPHEN WADE

Straightforward Publishing
www.straightforwardco.co.uk

Straightforward Publishing
Brighton BN7 2SH

© Stephen Wade 2011

ISBN 9781847161925

Printed by GN Digital Books Essex

Cover design by Bookworks Islington

Whilst every effort has been made to ensure that the information contained within this book is correct at the time of going to press, the author and publisher can take no responsibility for the errors or omissions contained within.

CONTENTS

1

PREPARATION FOR WRITING

This book provides a short introduction to all the aspects of writing skills which someone aspiring to be a freelance writer would need. This first chapter deals with the fundamental issues of what kind of writer you are, and what subjects might suit your interests and abilities best. Do the self-assessment exercises carefully and really think about the importance of them.

You as a reader and writer

If you are serious about becoming a writer who earns, and who has work in print rather than in a desk drawer, then this first subject is one you must consider now, before doing anything else. Every writer needs to know three basic things:

1. What should I write about?

2. Which language skills and styles are naturally for me?

3. How can I succeed, given my nature and skills?

The answer to these questions depends on whether you started writing in a constructive way. This means that you should ask some questions which may never have been asked before. These are the basic questions, with some pointers for you in your answers. Do the questionnaire diligently, and write a paragraph for each topic.

1. *Your autobiographical resources*
What aspects of your life-experience are potentially useful for writing?

(Consider your education, jobs done, hobbies, relatives, family history etc.)

2. *Your abiding interests*
What subjects do you find yourself most deeply interested in? For example, what areas of life and knowledge could you write about now - 'off the top of your head'?

(Consider your reading habits, topics of conversation etc.)

3. *Your imaginative nature*
What kind of imagination have you? Do you find yourself being fanciful about history when visiting an historical site? Do you daydream about certain places or people? (Think about any scenes from your past which constantly 'revisit' you in your fantasies or memories).

4. *You as an Observer*
What aspects of life and people do you spend time watching and noting? Do you notice detail?
(Reflect on how much you recall what people wear or say. Do you carry scenes in your head, so to speak?)

5. *Are you most interested in the past or in the future?*
Think about your habits of thought when you need to work on problem or a relationship - or even a particular event.

(Do you tend to look to past events for answers, or are you usually concerned with achievements to come, with aspiration?)

6. *Fact or fiction?*

Do you find that you are basically interested in information, statistics, scientific data etc. - or are you more interested in the imaginative expression of life? What types of reading would you instinctively choose for holiday reading? A biography, a novel or a dense piece of instructional prose?

All this is meant to make you stop and ask fundamental questions. The only area not covered here is that of language skills. It is assumed than you are proficient in writing clear and accurate English. If you feel that spelling or punctuation may be a weakness, attend to this now. Use a GCSE coursebook and revise these skills. They will be referred to in some of the exercises and case studies in later chapters.

After reflecting on this questionnaire, you should have some idea about these issues:

- Whether you are temperamentally suited to writing as creativity

- Whether you tend to analyse or respond

- Whether you put most attention on people or on ideas and abstractions

Essential Skills

The essential skills for freelance writing come under three areas:

1. Market involvement and interpretation

2. Using language for a set readership

3. Shaping a piece of writing to fit a given format and style

The first skill is about being aware of the publications in your subject-area. You should be sensitive to differences in various outlets which publish for your market. For instance, if you wanted to write pop music journalism, you should be a wide and regular reader of the magazines, and should know the differences in style and format between, for instance, *Select* and *New Musical Express*.

The second is about being able to produce the appropriate language and style for your selected publication. It might involve the use of particular slang and idiom, or writing sentences of a certain type or length.

The final skill is about drafting and editing what you do until it is definitely right for the market. This could involve writing a draft by enthusiasm and instinct first, then changing vocabulary and style to suit a pattern or an average stylistic format.

A Case Study: 'Model Writing'

A useful way to start thinking about these skills is to consider three different ways of writing about the same thing. Supposing that you have been asked to write a short book review on a novel. Look at these three variants:

(a)   John Smith's new thriller is anything but thrilling. It is supposed to be set in China in the years just after the second world war, and the idea is that the hero, an American mercenary gone right, is a hopeless romantic.

(b)   If you feel an instinctive dislike of people who kill for money, then you'll have problems with John Smith's latest hero.

(c)   Fiction these days has stalled in the doldrums of some post-romantic world of barrenness; where are we to look for originality - especially in genre fiction such as thrillers, in which tired old plots keep on appearing. John Smith's is one of these. A plot to make you yawn and long for the classics again.

It should be obvious what these represent. They show the factors involved in actually writing for very different outlets. The first appeals to regular readers of the genre. It fixes on people and place; the second is snappy, neat, calling on people who need a quick fix of fiction and they want guidance. The last one barely refers to Smith's novel. It's for the literary buff.

These are the kinds of distinctions to note and observe when you start out. A book review is one of the best ways to begin freelance work, and it is being used again to conclude this chapter, in order to make some basic points.

Think of your target reader

Supposing you start by attempting one of the most uncomplicated tasks: write a book review for your local newspaper, and offer to do so regularly. There must be several local evening papers which have no regular book column. Most will have the occasional review, usually a book by a local author or something similar. A useful first opening is this type of market. What considerations should you make? Here are some ideas.

Stage one. Think of length, style, readership and 'angle'

Stage two. Note these particulars. You might have -length: short. Say 300 words. An editor will look on this item as a 'filler'.

style: This outlet usually needs something chatty but informative. Certainly not academic and abstract.

readership: People not specifically interested in book information. A newspaper is about news! But you offer leisure - surely equally as important now?

angle: Inform and entertain. Bring out the fun in the reading. Only mention the positive.

The reader is the crucial factor here. Consider the methods at your disposal of finding out about the reader of any specified publication you might wish to write for.

The reference book:

A writers' publication such as *The Writers' and Artists' Yearbook* will give just a brief note such as ' for the amateur photographer' or 'specialist articles only'.

Specialist Magazines:

These offer the best advice. A magazine such as *Writing* gives updates on markets of all kinds.

Your own reading:

The best of all. If you read the publication regularly, you know by instinct what you want to read - so write for others like you. Register what it is you like.

Finally, remember that readers have different reasons for buying publications, and that the main reason is the common denominator, and is also decisive in the editorial decision as to whether or not to accept your article. Your review might be aimed at one of several readership groups, but if you start with a non-specialist group and think in terms of leisure, the net is wider.

Now read the KEY POINTS from chapter 1 overleaf.

KEY POINTS FROM CHAPTER ONE
PREPARATION FOR WRITING

- Assess your own disposition and interests, then relate these to your aspirations as a writer.

- Check your competence with the basic skills of language and market knowledge.

- Use a form of 'model' writing first, and base your first trial piece on that.

- Always consider the nature and needs of your hypothetical reader. Use all sources of information to define this reader's tastes

Now turn to Chapter Two

2

SURVEYING THE FREELANCE MARKETS

Now the groundwork is done, you should be in a position to investigate the existing outlets for freelance work. This chapter provides a survey of the range of options.

Range and options available

Having made the important decisions about exactly what you are capable of writing, and about who you want to write for, the subject of finding out what is available in the magazine and newspaper markets needs some thought. We live in an information-driven society. A quick scan of the shelves in any large newsagent will suggest the kind of markets which have opened out because of the need for people to be informed or entertained.

A constructive first step is to reflect on precisely what categories the magazine market embraces. This list summarises categories by means of some thought about the classes of readers.

1. Factual, specialist outlets.

2. Instructions for general readers

3. Leisure pursuits.

4. Creative, comic, anecdotal writing for general readers.
5. 'in-house' writing.

Notice that writing for a selected type from this list involves very careful and methodical study of the reader and his or her needs, as expressed in specific print outlets. That is, there is no point wasting your time by doing the following things as preparation:

- Writing 'blind' - not knowing the publication as a reader

- Using the wrong language and style - inappropriate for the readership

- Writing about topics which are too familiar or too abstruse.

It may seem obvious, but it happens all the time - a freelance just beginning on the path to print submits to an editor of a magazine which the writer has not seen and has never read. All that is available about the publication is a statement in the *Writer's and Artist's yearbook* that the magazine publishes 'humorous articles'. Clearly, the word humour can cover everything from political satire to anecdotes about cats and dogs.

Therefore, decide on your subject, your target readership and your approach to style. This is a useful checklist for such an enterprise:

<u>Subject</u>
Define particular aspects of a general subject

List topics for potential articles
Note which topics could be written on in several different ways for different outlets.

Readership

Think about age and interests
Note reasons for reading the target publication
Summarise aspects of style and language
Use a 'model' article

Approach to style

Start with a short piece, even a 'filler' in the style of a typical article for the outlet. Read aloud and absorb the intonation, sentence type etc.

Experiment with synonyms by using your thesaurus. E.g. would your target magazine prefer plenty of slang, detail or abstract ideas and stories?

Making an entrance

Now consider an example of a writer about to plan and submit the first article to a magazine. Our writer, John, knows a lot about the theatre. He has been involved in local theatre all his life, and he has taught drama in school and college. He has acted, and he knows a lot about scriptwriting, having produced pantomimes locally, together with a few sketches for reviews. John has taken early retirement and now wants to write as a hobby - but wants to earn something too.

Here is a suggested pattern of work, moving from his first planning to his first submission.

1. <u>Checklist of his current skills and knowledge</u>
acting and writing skills
production
examining and testing
organising and promoting events
costume
teaching drama

2. <u>Decisions about markets</u>
What magazines are in print and what do they publish?
- categories are teaching, amateur stage topics, national journals. learned journals.
- freelance openings seem to be in short news items, first-person experience and in critical analysis or factual items

3. <u>Range of publication forms</u>
These are:
glossy nationals for the arts generally
glossy specialist magazines
broadsheet format - amateur mostly
local and specialist publications

4. <u>Choice of target outlet</u>
John wisely decides that to start small and test the ground is the wisest choice. He decides on an idea for a series of articles on how to run a theatre group. The idea is to discuss all the practical tasks, skills and problems. He writes one article of 1,000 words and submits this, with a letter about the whole

idea, to a theatre magazine for all types of reader within amateur theatre.

John has done several wise and professional things in this process. He has researched the available outlets, selected a manageable goal and conceived of a rationale which would increase his chances of meeting a demand and actually offering more than a 'one-off' piece.

His first submission, with a letter, conveys three important communications to the editor in question.

1. Method

2. Clear knowledge of the subject

3. Relevant market research

An editor needs to know that a contributor knows and values the magazine in question; that the writer is at home with the house style and has a clear sense of who actually reads the publication, and why.

Professional help

Obviously, when starting out, there are some facts that need to be understood, and professional help is invaluable here. You do not want to waste time, money and energy in writing articles which have no market and have no sense of required style. Help means gaining access to the professional world. Notice that a careful reading of the handbooks about markets for freelance writing usually warn you off if there are no openings for outside writers. Words such as 'all material commissioned' or 'no submissions encouraged from first-time writers' will be included in the paragraphs of information for amateur writers.

The hard fact to absorb at this early stage is that entry into the national magazines is difficult and the competition fierce. You need to give your writing certain qualities from the very start. These are sharpness, appeal, relevance and sound basis in knowledge.

Our writer, John, with some persistence, would soon find that of ten magazines and newspapers which publish items on teaching and education, a few would be interested in publishing articles using his professional knowledge, but pay would be small - if there is any payment at all. So the earnings start to become potentially substantial only when John breaches a national publication, or is one of the lucky few who capture the imagination of the editor and the readers by sheer originality.

'Natural' writers are perhaps very rare. Most of us have to work hard to create a personal voice and style. Most freelance writing involves articles and profiles which merely describe, give facts and include some light relief. Dr. Johnson said that 'men more often need to be reminded than informed' and that explains the glut of articles based on the 'how to' principle which fill all the weekend magazines' leisure pages: cooking, fishing, antiques etc.

For these reasons, any professional help is very helpful. This can be found in these places:

Editors' responses
courses and tutors
critical services
writers' circles

These are dealt with in more detail in chapter 7. but the central point here is that you need such help with expending too much time or money. Very few busy editors will take the time to give you tips on how to improve your writing in order to meet their criteria for publication. The short answer is that you should use your local college or Workers' Educational Association and other similar organisations in order to meet other aspiring writers and to learn a range of basic skills.

Now read the KEY POINTS from Chapter Two

KEY POINTS FROM CHAPTER TWO
SURVEYING THE FREELANCE MARKETS

• Be aware of the options available in your subject area

• Research the range of outlets, and study the diversity in styles, readership groups and in-house policy and style.

• Plan your first submission in relation to your resources and also with links to a concept or series of related topics.

• Obtain as much professional help from educational courses and feedback groups as possible.

Now turn to Chapter Three

3

WRITING ARTICLES

Now we focus on the writing of an article. This involves being sure of the target publication and of the appropriateness of your style. The chapter also looks at ways of adopting a viewpoint and style for a selected readership.

Relevant surveys of markets

Freelance writing from scratch is clearly a difficult and challenging business, but it is not impossible to reach a stage where you have a steady trickle of articles finding publication outlets. You must plan now, at the beginning, and make it easier for yourself as you progress. One way of doing this is by researching your own market in some detail.

The best way to illustrate this is by example. Suppose our writer, John, wants to write an article on the subject of Pantomime. He should have a three-stage planning process before he puts pen to paper.

1. Select the publication which is most suitable for your subject. Actually read a copy - even if it has to be ordered by post.

2. Do a breakdown of the elements or ingredients of a typical article in that magazine. This might look like this:
(a) <u>Attitude or angle</u>

- informative but chatty, with personal experiences included, humorous - serious but not solemn.

- uses a basis of facts - costs, technical terms explained but used rarely

- no elaborate sentences or too many abstract words.

(b) <u>What does the reader want?</u>

- an easy read - armchair reading

- but a firm sense of having learned something practical

- no real intellectual or high art element - practical theatre.

3. <u>Sketch of the article;</u>

e.g. Panto - appeal, history, style, approach, type of humour, costume, examples of ones I have produced.

It would then be useful to write the first paragraph and read it aloud, alongside the opening of an article printed in the magazine. If you have a willing listener, they might be asked to guess which is from the magazine.

The markets available may cover several categories of course. Even the most trivial or specialist subject splits into sub-divisions. The knowledge-driven society embraces every subject imaginable. Just consider how many articles it would be possible to write on the subject of cooking for students in bed-sits for instance.

Perfect the style

This is the most difficult aspect of the subject. Freelance writing means that you should be able to write any one of a given range of styles within your catchment outlets. The basis of success in this is to ascertain *your own* natural style first. This checklist /questionnaire is to help you to gauge how flexible and versatile you might be in writing for a specified readership, rather than writing in your own natural way all the time.

Your own style?

1. Vocabulary

Do you tend to use a limited range of words in certain areas:
description - do you stress colour, size, shape or what?
images - are your images drawn from certain subjects - the sea, night, travel etc.
detail - do you tend to give attention to detail or write in broad generalities?

Do you tend to exclude foreign words and phrases - and why?
Would you use technical or abstruse words if they were accurate?

2. Sentences

What is the average number of words in your sentences?
Do you write about more than one subject in your sentences?
Do you digress?

3. Syntax
Do you always write in the same, natural English word order of subject-verb-object: example, *The player cleared the ball.*

4. Angle

Do you generally take up a certain stance or viewpoint on your subjects? (sarcastic, questioning, wry, factual, digressive, anecdotal?)

The only way to test this out is to write a paragraph in your natural manner, and then write on the same subject in the house-style of a selected magazine. Remember that *house style* has certain features:

• a sense of the reader that is very explicit

• a familiar humour

• a defined angle of view 'attitude to a shared subject

Perfecting your style, then, means practising the adoption of another way of writing - one that may not be natural to you. Here is an example of what might be involved:

Your natural style:
Organising a promotional event, like every type of organisation, requires careful planning, co-operation from people, and a clear sense of direction. The team involved needs to integrate and be aware what the joint objectives are.

The target style then might be, for instance, to say the same thing, but more like a conversation:

You need to work together when you're planning a promo. I mean, just think about the need to work together - if you can't get co-operation, you're finished.

Notice here how the notable difference is largely created by where each style is placed on a spectrum going from formal to informal:

formal...informal
precise, factual, specific chatty, like talk, relaxed, fun.

So there is a need to be aware of what aspects of language cause these nuances of meaning and expression. You might want to concentrate only on what you do best. For example, if you feel that you would never be able to adjust and write in ten slightly differentiated styles, then don't try - simply specialise in style as well as in subject.

Perfecting the style also means knowing your limitations. Nothing is so apparent as an attempt at a style which is patently not easy and assured from the writer's viewpoint. The fluency of what you write always has certain common factors, regardless of your adopted style. These factors for success might be listed like this:

- A sharing of the subject with the reader

- Enthusiasm and directness

- No talking down to the reader

- No display of facts for no identified reason

- Keep language contemporary

The fundamentals of successful article-writing involve being aware of the needs of the reader, and you can only do this by thinking like a reader yourself.

A useful piece of research at this point is to try this exercise, which is a simple analysis of an article:

1. Choose an article - on any subject- that you might read for leisure interest.

2. Assess the impact of the opening paragraph

3. Count and highlight the facts stated as opposed to the opinions

4. Rate the piece for page-turning quality (PTQ for short) on a scale of 1-10. A piece rated 10 should almost make you want to re-read.

5. Count the number of sentences and the number of technical or specialist terms used. Were they explained, and how well?

All this gives a reasonably accurate account of the success of an article in terms of sheer readability.

Monopolise on each idea

One valuable approach to work on, right from the start, is to make each topic you research and write about work for you in multiple contexts. That is, one article may easily be slightly edited and changed to suit a slightly different market. Consider a hypothetical example of a writer who wants to write on architecture, design, environment issues etc. He might research an old church, interview the vicar or a local historian. Before the interview (which is to be the basis of all the work) he plans three articles, all being variants of a basic piece on the architectural interest of the church:

1. Market: Specialist architectural magazine
angle and subject: stylistic features. The font, the misericordes etc.

2. Market: Local history:
angle and subject: the vicar and his interest in the church - how he went to work.

3. Market: Nostalgia and country magazine:
Human interest stories about the local people who have kept the church beautiful.

Obviously, there is a basis of just so many facts which are retained in each version, but with a word-processor, editing and re-writing are simple procedures. It would be mainly a matter of including less informal elements in the more general-reader oriented piece.

Monopolising also means finding the best outlet for each piece. You want to be able to adjust length, detail and so on according to the outlet in mind.

This is where you need the editing skills to reduce for word-length and style-changes. There are a few general guidelines here.

• Keep the editing process mainly to the sentence-work

• Make facts interesting

• Make a basis of facts work well- develop them fully.

• Include dramatic elements such as talk or action.

Finally, there are some very helpful practical steps you can take to maintain reference material. Keep the following to hand at your desk-side and update them:

A cuttings-book
This is made up of model articles - your favourite writers or 'classic' articles that really stand out as being excellent.

Quotations
Keep an index-book of quotations on your defined subject-area, for use in future articles. They liven up any piece of writing. File them under subjects which are easily accessible and which express themes you constantly write about.

Editor's responses
Keep any letters from editors that go beyond the curt 'No thank you'.

All these methods of preserving a sense of purpose, organisation and professionalism will pay off in the end. You are the only person who can impose this organisation, because no-one can write or plan exactly as you can. Every writer is unique in some way; you need to discover your own version of this uniqueness and then exploit it. Develop the skills you have most naturally in your language and style. These will be the ingredients of your articles that stand out in the editor's reading of your submission.

Now read the KEY POINTS from Chapter Three

KEY POINTS FROM CHAPTER THREE
WRITING ARTICLES

- Study your market carefully and analyse the qualities you must adopt in your style and language.
- Work methodically on writing the house style of your target publications. Read aloud and feel the individuality of each viewpoint.
- Make the most of each idea by writing up the piece into variants for markets in a narrow range of outlets.
- Keep reference material which will help with style and content.

Now turn to Chapter Four

4

THE CRAFT OF INTERVIEWING

The foundation of so much writing is an interview with a person who is a principal source of knowledge on a subject. Whether you want to write articles or profiles - or even main features - this is a valuable skill.

Preparation and requirements

First, it is important to define exactly what the uses of interviews are, and for what types of writing.

Factual articles/reportage
The interview may be with a witness to an event, or simply an expert in the field. Equally, it may be a strong human interest feature and you need first-person drama and witness.

Fiction
A personal statement of experience can be the basis of a story.

Profile
You may want to specialise in that category of writing that concentrates on profiles of people - basically, biographical writing mixed with journalistic technique.

Comedy/satire

Your thing might be social commentary or just sheer humour. A column or a regular review/gossip column might incorporate interviews.

The preparation involved is always the same, regardless of the type and reason. you need to research these aspects before you interview:

- any factual elements in the questions
- autobiographical facts that need to be avoided
- a summary of relevant contemporary data about the person

Then you need to decide on the form and angle you want to create from the interview notes. For instance, do you want to ascertain simply information about one specific event such as a flood or a fire they witnessed? Or are you wanting a human account of a wider experience such as a piece based on a person's work or achievements?

A checklist of questions to ask before you frame the interview will cover these things. It might look like this:

<u>Interview Preparation Checklist</u>

1. What do I want to know?
DATA
PERSONAL EXPERIENCE
OPINION ON............
2. What should the questions achieve?
FULL ANSWERS
SEARCHES FOR NEW INFORMATION

3. What should be avoided?

List irrelevancies, sensitive subjects etc.

Once you have done this, you need to think of just one more factor - the place and circumstances of the interview. A good interview must have these features: a workmanlike but informal atmosphere, assured communication and human interplay with a mood of directness and honesty. Therefore, questioning should not seem like a political interrogation; but neither should it be so relaxed that nothing happens. So the place and atmosphere are crucially important. You might consider these aspects:

- Indoors or outdoors?

- In the person's home or in a place significant to the topic?

- In easy chairs or quite formal?

- With accompanying food and drink?

There is also the question of whether or not to use intrusive equipment. But mainly, it is the interpersonal skills that help you most here. The non-verbal communication can win or ruin the day. As an interviewer, you need sensitivity to the interviewee's mood and character. This means that, although a set list of questions may have been prepared, you may have to adjust, change the order, re-state a question or omit one altogether. This all needs quick thinking and tact. As you make all this changes, you still need to keep the natural flow of the conversation going.

That is the heart of the matter - the interview should seem like a conversation, not an enquiry into a person's being.

Technical support

You may not always need any equipment. Some writers manage with a notepad and pen, coupled with a retentive memory. However, it is valuable to list some options and some pros and cons here. What are the options for support if you want to record and log the Q and A (question and answer) interplay?

portable tape-recorder
This may be very helpful. With an external microphone, though. Cheap ones often have an internal mike and there is too much motor-noise when in playback. The advantage is that it looks professional. The respondent feels as though the process is 'like on t.v.'

micro-cassette recorder
This is the one that fits in your pocket. They can cost only £30 or so, and are very useful indeed. The respondent hardly notices the machine, which can be placed on a table or chair-arm if you are in a relaxed atmosphere. Obviously, never hold it close to the person's face. What you must ensure is that you are in a quiet place with no significant background-noise, though. Such intrusions provide a scratch or a rumble which can block out the voice in replay.

Video camera/camcorder
Obviously, unnecessary, but if you have reasons, and the person is happy with that, then go ahead.

Of course, if you know shorthand, then things are so much easier. But for most of us, the ideal method is to concentrate on the questions and the give and take of the conversation, so we need something that will record everything without intruding on the scene.

Ways of working

There are several ways of going about the subtle and intricate process of interviewing someone. Basically, you either ask short questions and allow lengthy, digressive and anecdotal answers, or you provoke, explore and reinforce by using strings of related questions and inviting more amplification where you need it.

In practical terms, this means one of these two options: each one has its good and bad points, and you should use the one that suits your character, because you must remember that you are involved in a two-way process. An interview is not an analysis session.

Method one
Ask simple and direct questions, note the answers and proceed only when the person has stopped.

Method two
Ask longer, more searching questions, building on them if the answers are not what you want.
Examples:

Method one might be: 'How did you feel about working in the vice squad?'

The Q and A might be:

A All right. You felt you were doing something.

Q Better than the general detective work?

A Not really.

Method two presses and develops:

A All right

Q Just all right? No more?

A Well, good pay. You were valued.... it was demanding work.

The only important aspects of working methods are the establishment of rapport and fluency, and the consideration for the respondent. Given those two factors, you can work with either approach, as long as you can access the information afterwards.

Notes after the event

This is the time-consuming part. You have done the interview and gone home. What do you have to work on? A notebook of scribbles or maybe a 90-minute cassette which has to be replayed and notes extracted? Think about each process:

1. *Notebook*

With this, you might have six pages of headings and lists, with phrases taken verbatim from the respondent - in other words, a jumble. So you need to take a highlighter and pick out all useful points, then rank them by number in order of importance for use in the article.

2. *Tape*

Now, this is time-consuming. You have to sit, with headphones on, and extract the phrases or facts you wish to use. The exercise is all about the pause and replay buttons, of course, but it if often found with this process that you tend to select more easily, and with a sense of editing on the spot, so to speak.

Good and bad questions

The traditional categories of open and closed questions apply here as in every account of conversation. Remember that a closed question allows only for a yes/no answer:

Q You liked the work?
A Yes.
An open question invites amplification of the topic:

Q How did the work compare to the time in the army?
A Much better.... you earned more and had some time alone.

But poor questions can also be put when these things happen:

Long, complex questions - the clumsy and muddled syntax of some questions leaves the respondent feeling unsure of what has been asked.
Vague questions: for example 'So..what?' or 'Then you....?'

Now read the KEY POINTS from Chapter Four.

KEY POINTS FROM CHAPTER FOUR
THE CRAFT OF INTERVIEWING

- Prepare carefully and be sure of what you want to come away with.

- Decide on recording methods and think through the practicalities.

- Consider the notes you will have to use afterwards.

- Plan and pre-design your questions, making sure that they will ascertain exactly what you want from the session.

Now turn to Chapter Five

5

SPECIALIST OR ALL-ROUNDER?

As decisions about how you are to work are made, and as a clearer idea emerges of what sort of subjects you wish to write about, a point comes at which a writer needs to make a decision about specialisation. This chapter is about how and why you must build and progress.

Narrowing your range

As you progress and start developing your expertise, and hopefully get to know some editors, you begin to be noted as a writer who is linked with certain subjects. In other words, you are defined and 0compartmentalised.

Imagine that an editor wants a piece on theatre from our imaginary John. He may well, after three years, have written about the same thing for a dozen different outlets. John may be quite happy with that - or he may wish that he had worked on a wide range from the outset.

Charles Handy, the business guru, has a concept of 'portfolio work'. By this he means that in today's labour market, people need a string of job-skills, a spectrum of skills. The same might be said of writing. There are rewards for both routes, but consider these two lists:

Specialist
Potentially, could progress to more than local or specialist outlets. Reputation as an expert might assure a demand.

Easier to keep on top of your subject: files updated easily etc.

The internet has made research easier.

Generalist
Able to offer diversity
Not labelled.
Open to new developments
Wider range of outlets - but at the basic level.

Suppose you are a student, thinking of a career in writing or journalism. As a freelance, you could relate your writing topics to your degree programme as well as to your leisure interests. If you are studying modern languages, for instance, your potential subjects could range from European issues to translation of fiction; from interviews with artists from France or Germany to features on exchange students in England. There would be a variety of potential outlets for all these.

In other words, every writer needs to work out a plan for optimum use of experience, writing skills and future markets. A freelance needs to forecast trends in subject-interest. The more subjects you have, the more chances of accurate prediction.

If you do narrow your range, then, how is it to be done? The simple answer is that you look for diversity within the topic area. Suppose you write on food and drink. Take the broad area and list divisions which relate to different types of readers: e.g. Italian wine:

General outlet types: in-flight magazines, weekly supplements, wine magazines, European publications.
Then use the reference books to find the variety of publications within each category. You could collect twenty outlets.

organisation
All this thinking and planning demands excellent organisation. A positive suggestion is to have a master file with all subjects indexed clearly, and with sub-headings. If we stay with food and drink, then imagine a heading on ITALY: WINE, then sub-headings alphabetically, covering anything from festivals to folklore or even wine for health.

Why are you writing?

All this hinges on one important question - why are you writing? If you are relying on writing as a source of extra income, or spending money, then specialism may increase your chances of holding a regular outlet. You might, for instance, write for a national magazine or professional publication on just one area - say law for teachers - if an editor likes what you do, then he or she has your name on file and will want regular contributions.

On the other hand, if you want writing to be your career, then you might consider books and writing for television and radio.

If you have all day to write, then you also have more time for networking and promotion, of course.

Ask yourself these questions at this point, when you have perhaps written your first articles or features:

1. Am I serious about acquiring all the necessary skills?

2. Am I prepared to make a commitment to a defined period and see if I succeed within that time?

3. Am I receptive to the idea of attending courses etc. for writing?

4. Am I genuinely reading and learning from the writer who have succeeded and whom I admire?

The besetting sins of writing freelance are over-confidence and naivety. Never assume that editors are clamouring for your work. The competition is massive and there is a lot of talent around. Do not be naive enough to think that you can compete immediately with the full-time professionals. You have to put everything into your first article and submit to a realistic market, with a good covering letter. If you are sure of why you are writing, then these will all be more attainable.

There is also the pleasure factor. If you log your responses to writing and to feedback received, both in success and rejection, then the enjoyment of writing and the sheer irresistible urge to write must be somewhere in that monitoring process. If not, think honestly and long before continuing. There is a great deal of stress in rejection.

For ambition or income - or both?
There is an important point to be made here about the different strategies involved in freelance writing, depending on these ultimate aims. For instance, if you are prepared to allow for a 'warming up' period in which you establish yourself as a 'name' in your area, then this might pay off in the long term. If part of your ambition is to see your name in print - and that this is the first consideration, before starting to earn, then there are some aspects of this which are worth noting at this stage.

A three-stage plan
You might allow for the fact that, as you are not a known name as a writer, you need the platform of publication first - *any* publication. If this is so, then this plan seems to make sense:

1. Get into print - even if there is no payment involved. Write for professional publications or in local newspapers - even college magazines - and count this as establishing a portfolio. You will then have a track record as a writer. Treat your writing as being similar to an art student's portfolio of sketches.

2. Promote yourself well and distribute your printed work along with submissions to larger publications.

3. Then consider yourself a small business, in effect. That is what you are.

All this makes sense in a world where a complete beginner has very little chance of success alongside established names; so you must ask yourself the question, what turns a newcomer into an established name?

Monitoring your ultimate aims

This is all about logging progress and ensuring that you are on course towards the goals you set yourself at the outset. A good recommendation is to write the initial goals in a record-book and list all acceptances, successes, courses attended and so on. The goals might be something like this:

At the end of year 1 -
Approach a selection of editors with ideas and drafts of articles

Establish an identity as a writer
by year 2-

Have six articles in print in any outlet.
Expect to earn a figure in the hundreds.

by year 3 -
Article(s) in nationals!
Why not top the thousand mark in earnings?
In addition, you could list the target publications in this logbook.

Be realistic
It might seem that the above aims relate only to very moderate ambitions, and that it seems to be just a hobby. Well, for most

writers, that is what it is. The hard fact is that, unless you find a real 'gap' in the market that expands and demand for more work is always on your doorstep, then progress will seems very moderate from the beginning. Being realistic does not necessarily mean being small-scale.

If you do specialise, that will often mean that your work is circulated; communication by word of mouth may start to bring in more approaches and commissions. Everything depends on how broad your base of operations is; if you restrict submissions to one medium, obviously, your options are limited. In other words, if you write on current affairs or social issues, then why not write for radio - local and national - in addition to writing for magazines? Why not write for foreign markets as well as the domestic ones?

Overall, success depends on how well you work out your rationale when you set about finding a modus operandi - a way of working that suits your time and resources.

Now read the KEY POINTS from Chapter Five

KEY POINTS FROM CHAPTER FIVE
SPECIALIST OR ALL-ROUNDER?

- Make decisions about the scope of your work - how widely to aim in terms of your defined subject-matter.

- Be absolutely clear about your reasons for writing and monitor these aims.

- Write down your goals for a set period and specify publications targeted.

- Take account of the status of a beginner entering a well-trodden ground for operations, and do not expect immediate success. Set a time-period.

Now turn to Chapter Six.

6

YOU AND THE EDITOR

Now that the guidelines for planning and methodical work have been discussed, there is a need to think about submission of work for consideration by an editor.

A case study

A neat way to illustrate the nature of a good writer-editor relationship is to describe a case study. Imagine our writer, John, has now had his first acceptance from the editor of a drama magazine. How can this situation be developed for everyone's benefit? Think about what the writer and editor want from this initial success.

John has proved that he can deliver quality work which suits the readership of the magazine. Here are some relevant points from both angles:

writer
John has succeeded. He knows that he can do it and maybe do it again.

He wants, ideally, to secure a situation which might entail being commissioned to write more. He is prepared to change and adapt if necessary.

editor

The editor knows that he has a writer on his list who can handle a particular topic well - but this is a one-off occasion. So he wonders whether John can diversify.

He wants a writer who is one of a 'pool' of resources to call on.

He wants versatility but also reliability in all contributors.

John should react to the success in a specific way. HE has to make it clear that he has lots of resources to call upon, and that he is eager to continue. He needs to make it clear that he is very useful to the magazine, and is willing to go along with the in house needs.

The writer can do several things which will help the cause:

• supply examples of other articles from the files

• summarise potential topics he /she would like to cover in future

• give essential information from his/her c.v. which may hint at potential work.

Remember that the first letter which was enclosed with the very first submission did not have a full c.v.

Now is the writer's chance to give more information - details which would have seemed irrelevant to the editor on receiving the first submission.

Good practice and good manners

This is the ideal time to define what the editor of a magazine or radio features department needs from a freelance. Above all else, it is these things:

- reliability

- a defined area of expertise

- a recognised style - something individual in the words

- a professional approach to submission

- good research and preparation skills

These are all essential aspects of the relationship. Good practice from the writer means being able to meet deadlines and to produce the right subject and style for the publication. You need to have a 'feel' for what the reader wants. On the practical side, you need to be prepared to edit and re-write if need be, and also to investigate new subjects if the editor feels that you would suit that.

Good practice should also be expected from the editor also. The writer wants to depend on someone who is honest and approachable, but also professionally aware of the constraints upon the work in hand. As long as the writer provides suitable work, on time and of the desired length and style, there should be rewards for the writer. The importance of these aspects of the relationship should be mentioned here:

1. The contract or agreement being defined.

2. Explicit statements about fees given.

3. Prompt payment of the above.

4. Facts about who own copyright of the text.

5. Information about amendments required.

Notice that the important topics of payment and copyright have now entered our vocabulary. These are crucial to you as a freelance. Obtain written statements about payment offered and copyright destinations before agreeing to publication. General rates for freelance work are listed annually in Barry Turner's *Writer's Handbook* (Macmillan), but in most cases, you will have to negotiate. Decide in your own mind what payment you consider apposite for the work done. The time spent in research as well as in writing should be taken into account. Copyright is usually retained by the author in most cases, but an editor should tell you - and in print - if there are any rights relinquished by you when you sign an agreement to publish. Again, Barry Turner gives the up-dated facts every year. His book should be on your writer's bookshelf, along with the dictionary and thesaurus.

A working partnership
Think of the editor-writer communication process as a working partnership. The ideal is co-operation. When you absorb what aspects of writing may be involved in the editing and submission work, you realise how important this is. For

instance, imagine that you have submitted an article to a magazine. Then, you receive a reply from the editor :

Dear Contributor,
Many thanks for your article on resources for geography teachers. I think that this is, potentially, of real interest to readers of Classroom Business and I would like to use it in my regular Chalkface column.

However, as it stands, it isn't quite right for that. Could you reduce the piece to around 300 words? It would also need the technical terms explaining - such things as metamorphic rock etc.

Do let me know if you are happy to do this.
Yours etc.

Notice that, in the first response, there is no talk about payment or copyright. The important job is to cut the cloth to fit the person. The editor wants you to meet certain specifications. What does the writer do?

Obviously, if you want the piece to see print, you do the following:

• edit down to the words required

• find a way of explaining the terms - incorporated into text etc.

• ensure that the style and angle match the *Chalkface* format.

The editor will learn several important things about you if you respond promptly and accurately in this task. He/she will learn that you are reliable, skilful enough to adapt to in house needs, and that you can produce the right style for a specific feature of the publication.

When the re-write is accepted, then you talk money and copyright. Note here that some publications have a standard sheet which you sign, agreeing to a sum in payment and to copyright conditions. Others will simply say that they accept your piece and nothing else happens unless you right and clarify things.

Problems!
Sometimes, there is friction in the relationship. The causes are usually in these categories:

- delay in publication

- delay in payment

- poor communication

- cuts and changes made in your text without consultation

In many cases, little can be done about this. All you can do is write, remind and be firm in what you ask for. If you encounter bad manners and inefficient or rude editors, then cross their name off your list and leave it behind you.

Submission of work and re-writing

As mentioned above, when you are asked to edit a piece, it may entail some hard re-thinking and will test your language skills to the utmost. But the first step is to be sure about what constitutes a professional submission of work to an editor. Here is a checklist of what should be included in this:

1. A short covering letter.

2. The text, not stapled and in a folder.

3. Good margins around the text

4. Brief career details - a mini- c.v. in fact

5. A self-addressed stamped envelope.

The covering letter
This should be short - only a few paragraphs:

Dear editor,
Please note the enclosed article which I would like to submit for consideration: could it be suitable for your readers? I was trying here to produce something chatty but informative, and I feel that your magazine has that character.

I have written on this subject previously, but this is my first submission to you. I enclose a stamped, addressed envelope for the return of the script etc.

Yours faithfully,

Notice the exactness and lack of any digression whatsoever. Brief and businesslike is the aim.

Career details

Again, these should be in the form of a few paragraphs or a list, stating just the achievements which may be relevant to the specific outlet you are aiming at. You might refer to other publications and projects, work experience or any study you have done which is relevant.

Re-writing

As mentioned earlier in this chapter, a writer needs to edit and re-write on most occasions. It is useful here to list the skills involved. The exercise is a trial of your ability with language, and involves a process of selection and rejection. For instance, supposing you have to re-write this paragraph to a more formal style:

The point about studying a foreign language is that a lot of it is lonely and dull. It's just you and a book or a cassette, and you repeat everything until you want to shout for help. A language asks for total concentration.

You might erase phrases and replace with single, precise words:

You study texts and recordings / it can be frustrating working by yourself etc.

But a re-write is the real test of your resolve as well. The only way to win is to practise; take any few paragraphs from an article which you might write, and re-express as if for a different publication.

This is the best training for the real test when it comes along. The obvious way to grasp the stylistic range is to read three of four publications on the same subject and note the features of:

sentence length
technical terms
abstract words
address to the reader

Now read the KEY POINTS from Chapter Six

KEY POINTS FROM CHAPTER SIX
YOU AND THE EDITOR

- Operate in a professional way from the start

- Be prepared to adapt to varying demands that editors may ask of you.

- Set out to be certain about the terms of publication - copyright and payment details should be written down and kept to.

- Be prepared to edit and re-write your texts and practise the skills involved in these processes.

Now turn to Chapter Seven

7

NETWORKING AND PROMOTION

It is now time to pay some attention to the promotional and developmental aspects of being a writer who earns. This includes the difficult matter of self- development and adding a public dimension - coming out of the study - if you wish to do so.

Workshops

One way of extending your writing career beyond simply writing at your desk day after day is to consider taking part in writing workshops. Why do this? A workshop is a one-day session on an aspect of writing and it may lead you to learn more about the skills you need to progress. A workshop is usually run by an experienced and widely-published writer, so there will be a lot to learn. The benefits can be enormous. You simply need to decide what aspect of writing you want to improve, then search out the workshop. These are some of the main advantages of attending them:

- tuition by a professional teacher/writer

- meeting contacts in your field - good networking

- concentration on one defined aspect of the work

- interchange of ideas and a chance to ask questions

- market knowledge

Notice that these are all related to the notion of making your presence felt. That is, contrary to the popular myth, writing is not totally about a lonely dedication to covering the screen of your PC every day, working factory hours. That is hackwork. It is just as important to meet other writers, editors, tutors and readers. A typical workshop would take this form:

Topic: Writing effective documentary/reportage
Meeting/coffee/introductions
Speaker - the features of documentary - history and styles
question time
lunch
Speaker- practising writing a treatment
smaller groups for writing
coffee and conclusion

Note that the planning almost compels writers to mix, communicate - and to write with others, comparing approaches.

Courses

Attending a course is a different matter. A course implies a complete and structured series of classes on writing. But remember that there is a real diversity of courses now, offering tuition at all levels, for beginners and for published writers. If you are a beginner, you might want to consider which of the courses available suits you best. The options are:

- short full-time courses on media or on freelance/creative writing.

- part-time leisure courses (often for a set number of weeks)

- part time vocational courses

- distance learning/ correspondence courses

Whatever commitment you make in time and energy, the main point is that you should make every effort to assess the benefits to you, in the context of your career-planning. For instance, a course might be on Writing Science Fiction or on Research methods for Writers.

Notice that one type is actively language-based; the latter is a general skill for all types of writers. Which do you need most and which could you learn more easily from a textbook? The most important factor is in whether you are going to absorb a transferable skill.

Often, a short course taught by a professional, such as an Arvon course (see the last chapter) may be more beneficial than a six-week course at the local further education college. Only you can assess the potential value of what is on offer. Go and talk to people and write letters of enquiry. Collect brochures and syllabuses.

Readings

This word conjures up just one type of writing - poetry. But, in fact, a reading can be anything, based on all types of writing, if you plan it well. A reading makes an ideal promotional event. You might, for instance, get to know local poets in writing groups, and offer to work with them. You may simply write about them, of course. But why not participate, reading some of your own work, or even talking about your writing. The main audiences would be writing groups and arts groups, of course. The real reason for this is making contacts and opening doors: networking again.

Clubs and societies

This is the point at which you start to become national and truly professional. The question is: is it worth your while to join a professional group such as a society of writers or an organisation related to your sphere of interest? The possibilities are quite wide. These are some of the principal categories:

- a national organisation such as P.E.N. or The Society of Authors.

- a society restricted to one type of writing such as the Comedy Writers' Circle or the Poetry Society

- a society which actively promotes events and meetings such as the local art associations

Each type has its own type of benefit for a freelance.

For example, suppose you decide that you really want to network, be involved in literature festivals, work in schools and colleges, edit magazines and so on, then arts associations and writers' circles will be for you. Take a typical example of a freelance writer who, like very many, has a wide spectrum of interests.

Mr. Anon, writer, has had his details printed in the writers' directory of his nearest Arts Association.

It might look like this:

John Anon
Interests: short stories, articles, journalism.
Publications: Mainly feature articles in magazines and radio features. Stories in anthologies.
Offers: Workshops in college, mainly for adult students. Readings interested in festival bookings.

What stands out here is the flexibility; anyone wanting John for an event would note that they had someone who could easily fit in with a group project, or fill in a spot in a programme quite easily.

But societies also offer something which is priceless: they give you an opportunity to mix and talk shop; to exchange ideas and perhaps find someone to collaborate on projects with you. They also offer publication in most cases, even on a small scale. The Humberside Writers' Association, for example, have produced two anthologies of writing since they were formed a few years ago.

You as a company

What should be apparent by now is that a freelance writer is a company - a one-person outfit. The writer has to be a skilled organiser. Just think how you need the basics at your disposal. This might be a checklist of essential organisational factors for your promotion and identity as a freelance:

1. Most important - a PC and filing systems.

2. A quiet, organised space to work in.

3. Record-keeping methods for logging work sent and in production.

4. regular up-dating of publication details.

5.Access to research sources and good reference books.

6. Contacts in your special areas of writing expertise.
You are aiming to be independent and to appear efficient, professional and well-informed. The obvious trappings of a small company should also be produced; a business-card, a logo and letterheads. Your diary-keeping is the hub of everything. The answerphone will, hopefully, earn its keep. Most of all, you will be always adding to your circle of contacts. A basic list of records for research material and monitoring work might be:

- A log of work submitted and responses from editors
- An index of drafts being worked on

- A file of cuttings to be developed and used
- Any interview transcripts, catalogued
- A c.v. always up-to-date.

Now read the KEY POINTS from Chapter Seven

KEY POINTS FROM CHAPTER SEVEN
NETWORKING AND PROMOTION

- Investigate the workshops available for improving writing in specific categories and for set markets.

- Decide whether you might benefit from a course in writing - particularly the ones which offer commercial or transferable skills.

- Consider joining a society, for networking and for expanding your knowledge of your markets.

- Work on your identity as a freelance - a business image is essential, with attention paid to all aspects of records and monitoring of progress.

Now turn to Chapter Eight.

8

DEVELOPING FURTHER

By now, having organised yourself as a writer who means to sell work and operate as a freelance business, decisions will have been reached about what subjects and approaches to specialise in. This chapter looks at some common examples of freelance specialisms.

Beginning to specialise

The point about settling on your areas of interest as a writer is that it offers several advantages with regard to keeping that necessary flow of supply and demand from publication to writer. These advantages are:

- knowing with certainty an editor's requirements

- having easy access to changing or new publications

- being able to use material in a range of outlets

Notice that these points all refer to a routine and a comfortable link between publication sources and writing expertise. A case study will illustrate these advantages even more clearly. Let us imagine that John, our writer on drama and education, has now established a variety of markets, relating to a range of different forms and styles. His list of publications might look something like this:

publication	material	styles etc.
Playing Theatre 1,000 wds.	factual, profiles	formal,
Dramatic Themes 500 wds.	concerned with teaching	chatty
Green Room Notes from critical to chatty .	interviews with actors etc.	varies

Note that this keeps a check on changes also; John would log any changes due to format, audience or house policy as a publication grew and responded to market needs. Equally, the art of using one article for three outlets, with slight changes made to vocabulary and style, could be reflected in this. Three publications out of twenty might be interested in the same topic. Small changes or additions to each would make them into three separate ones.

Writing for a genre

Now for the first example of a popular specialism. A genre is simply a category of writing, with its own conventions of style, treatment and language. A simple example would be the short story in the genre of love and romance. What types of organisation, planning and writing would be needed here? This is a suggested approach.

stage one
Research the existing magazine, radio and newspaper outlets. List and describe the obvious features such as length, number of characters, viewpoint, common settings etc.

You might have a range covering 1,000-word family romance, to 4,000 word stories with exotic settings or with a historical subject. There are also openings for novella-length stories (short novels in paperback form)

stage two
summarise the features more precisely, and select which type best matches your interests and abilities. For instance, you might decide on stories which are more raunchy, for modern young women, or on more family-oriented relationships based on older people falling in love. The idea of a holiday romance, for instance, is something that has infinite variations in style. You might plan this in this way:

1.   Characters - early twenties, quite well off, looking for excitement etc.

2.   Settings - abroad. A holiday club, Mediterranean hotels.

3.   Themes - sheer pleasure, escapism, thrills of romance etc.

Writing in a genre means that you try your best to find an original angle but keep to a presentation which relates to the common way of writing. Different publications will have varying attitudes as to what extent they expect writers to give them predictable storylines. In westerns, for instance, the outlets are limited in Britain, and even if you plan to write novels, the number of publishers is very small, and some are hidebound by a very restricted, narrow view of what constitutes a western.

stage three

Now it's time to try your first genre piece and find out how skilful you are. Submit to selected magazines first, and also send samples of fiction to an agent. You need to explain what niche in the overall market you feel the work aims at. In romance, for instance, notice that a quick survey of the classifications used by Harlequin Mills and Boon embraces medical, historical and contemporary romance.

From articles to books?

A point will arrive when you might want to make the transition from short articles or stories to book-length material. A typical scenario would be a writer who has established a local reputation writing a column, then advanced into more sustained feature-writing and been published in a few nationals. He has a small reputation in his chosen area. One day, it occurs to him that twenty articles or stories might make a book that would sell reasonably well.

What thinking is needed here is determined by the reasons for branching out. A book with a small publisher might develop a writer's reputation, simply give some prestige, and so make the next book more of a proposition. The point is that an unknown author is always a risk. If a small publisher receives a typescript of perhaps two hundred pages of fiction, what is the response likely to be? These would be the typical ones:

- Is this writer known to the general public?

- Is the writing original enough or with intrinsic merit?

- Is the subject topical, easily definable by genre etc?

- Would direct sales be possible – readings/workshops etc?

These points illustrate the boldly commercial elements in publishing which are obviously the ones that will determine the reception you receive when you submit text or proposal.

So there is a method of moving from into writing books which will maximise your chances of success. This is the process:

1.   Study the market for your chosen topic and assess what exists

2.   Compare the closest competitive title to the format of the one you want to write and make your difference obvious.

3.   Write a proposal, outlining your book: aims, style, market etc.

4.   Write and submit the first chapter. (Fiction - three chapters)

Remember that the large publishers (mostly in London) will have lists which are full for some time ahead, and that they have a string of established authors. Essentially, you should offer something that is clearly lucrative at least in potential, and also make it clear that you know what you are talking about.

Using an agent

There is an on-going debate about whether or not first-time authors should use an agent. Basically, this springs from the general process of submission and reading of scripts at publishers. What would happen if you sent a full-length novel or factual book to a large publisher? Usually, the book, as it would be from an unknown, would be read by a junior editor, after being left for some time on the 'slush pile' of unsolicited manuscripts. Then, if there was any chance that the editor thought there was enough originality and writing power, it would be read again by someone more senior. The depressing fact is that virtually all such submissions are returned.

Using an agent means that first of all you have to secure an agent's interest. This is where the original organisation and steady publishing 'track record' you have worked on starts to pay dividends. Imagine that John has now written thirty articles and interviews on theatre and he wants to write a book on teaching drama for teachers. Here is his plan of action:

- Research the specific market

- Find an agent who deals with that subject

- Also send samples to relevant publishers

- Explain the target reader and use of the book.

John would find that his actual writing style and the commercial viability would be the decisive factors in this case. His writer's c.v. would be a very useful piece of support-material as well. Publishers of factual and informative books obviously want writers with professional and relevant experience, and a proven ability to write for the designated readership.

The decision of whether or not to use an agent in the end depends on what the agent offers to do, once an interest in your work has been expressed. The obvious advantages are that the agent knows people in the publishing industry relating to your subject and knows publishable quality. After all, it is to their advantage to see your work into print, as they take a percentage of all profits made.

There are plenty of examples of writers who have succeeded on their own simply submitting typescripts to publishers. But an agent is not the only alternative. You can also use critical services, join writers' groups and even self-publish as a commercial enterprise.

Now read the KEY POINTS from Chapter Eight

KEY POINTS FROM CHAPTER EIGHT
DEVELOPING FURTHER

- Work out the practicalities of specialising and organise your targets with a clear sense of the markets available.

- If and when you write for a specific genre, research the format, styles and conventions thoroughly and choose a 'slot' in the overall market.

- When progressing from shorter forms to books, plan a new approach or provide essential subject-matter within an existing market and defined readership.

- Consider the pros and cons of using an agent, learning about the publishing process first and sampling the existing publishers first.

Now turn to Chapter Nine.

9

YOUR RESOURCES AND RESPONSIBILITIES

The focus now shifts to the practical matters of using all available resources to make your writing life smooth, regulated and purposeful. Also, there is a firm need to consider networking and promotion of your work.

Books and magazines

Every freelance needs a shelf of reference books, and you should decide how to store and use these according to categories. This is the basic checklist, with uses:

Dictionaries: general and subject-centred.
These could include the following - dictionary, thesaurus, dictionary of terminology, biographical reference etc.

Handbooks and professional directories
These could include addresses of contacts, businesses, geographical information etc. Also, directories of writers such as the ones published by professional societies and arts associations.

Books on markets, language, writing technique.
This includes books such as this one, along with one of the two standard writing reference books:

Barry Turner   *The Writer's Handbook*   (Macmillan, annual)

A&C Black (publishers) *The Writers' and Artists' Yearbook*

In addition to these, you might need a handbook on your own specific type of writing. There are hundreds available, ranging from science fiction to writing on cookery.

Magazines:
The two most widely-circulated and respected magazines are important for updated information about publishers as well as being excellent for the expert advice they offer on style and technique. These are:

Writing Magazine PO Box 4, Nairn, Scotland IV 12 4HU

Writers News (as above)

There is another use of magazines and books as reference tools, and this is to develop a system of alphabetically-arranged files and cuttings relating to your markets and readership. This is an extension of the topic dealt with earlier in Chapter Two.

The media as your friend

These days, when you publish a book, you receive information from the publishers on how you can help to promote your work. The old habits of the writer producing the book and then the publisher doing everything else have gone. There is so much competition now for shelf-space (and shelf-life) that you need to promote your work -whether in books or in any other media - yourself.

These are the basic promotional methods which are easily available to a writer:

- local radio. Arrange an interview about your work when something new appears.

- local newspapers. As above

- Networking: use established circles of colleagues in writers' groups.

- Readings - have a useful address-list of local contacts such as the organiser of classes in adult education.

Never forget that the media are looking for a contemporary or topical angle on anything! Look for and promote any aspect of what you write about that may be significant, entertaining or just simply timely regarding social events and news.

There are also the regional arts associations. The literature officer for your area has a responsibility to be supportive to you, and to supply you with information about other writers and writing events. Some of them publish regular arts diaries and from these publications, you can build up your network of organisers and fellow-writers.

Personal files

Hopefully, certain very helpful habits of work and attitudes will develop from these activities. If they do, you then have the question of how to organise your personal information-sources. Here is a suggestion.

1. *Keep three separate notebooks/diaries*
(a) Addresses of editors and organisers
(b) Addresses of writers in your field.
(c) Up-dated details of courses, groups and publications.

2. *Keep an on-going c.v. and add to it at the end of each month.*

This would include-
courses attended
people met at meetings etc.
everything published are in which publication
all P.R. activities undertaken.
involvement in readings/workshops.

3. *Planning*
List all intended work, from writing projects to self-development, with deadlines.

Financial records
This topic is very important. If you are writing merely as a sideline, obviously, the taxation element in affairs has to be attended to. If you are going full-time, professional, then tax and basic bookkeeping is perhaps more important.

Ideally, you need an accountant, but until you are wealthy enough to employ one, just ensure that you do these chores regularly and with a system:

1. Log all relevant expenses and outgoings, along with all income. Keep receipts. Include stationery, office equipment, books, research and travel costs. The tax handbooks such as the one issued by Lloyds Bank have essential information about allowable expenses.

2. If you are using a room at home as an office, you may claim a proportionate amount of tax relief based on the premise that the room is a place of work. (Heating, lighting etc. considered)

3. Be meticulous about travel. Log everything, such as a journey to interview someone or to a library. Specify rail or car travel etc.

Above all, when starting out, expect to make a loss or a small profit at first, and use a long-term plan, aiming at a steady trend towards profits. Set a trial period and decide on targets.

Now read the KEY POINTS from Chapter Nine

KEY POINTS FROM CHAPTER NINE
YOUR RESOURCES AND RESPONSIBILITIES

- Use reference books and magazines as support material and always have printed sources of professional data and contacts available.

- Organise promotion of your work, with a positive attitude, and make approaches to all local media to promote your latest writing.

- Keep accurate records, financial and practical, on all aspects of the day-to-day working practices of your chosen subject-area.

Now turn to Chapter Ten.

10

A SUMMARY AND AN INITIAL EXERCISE

In this last chapter, the aim is to crystallise everything that has been said, mainly by going through an exercise from idea to submission, using a short article for a magazine.

Aim at a slot.

Above all else, when you write for a specified market, be sure of the nature of the 'slot' you see. Whether you aim at a five-minute radio feature/talk or at a short story of 800 words with a 'twist in the tale', the basis of success is how close your work is to the identity of the set piece, in house style and intention.

What determines the identity of a particular placing could be any of these:

- expected readership response

- placing in the format (light relief? serious bit?)

- writer-prominence (do the readers want the writer first, words after?)
- topical re-adjustments.

The point to reflect on here is what the target piece you are writing is trying to do: entertain? provide debate? simply tell an anecdote? Let's work on a specific example.

An example 'target' article

Suppose we are to write a 500 word piece for a typical 'opinion column' that open to freelance writers. Newspapers often have such a column and invite experts in the field to contribute. Our example is to be a topic on education.

The challenge is simply to write on any educational topic and begin a debate. The publication would like readers to reply.

The task
To write a strongly argued article, with references to experience or facts, without pomposity, talking-down or grumbling.

Angle?
Intelligent, modern, informed, like a coffee-break conversation in which someone expresses a point well, succinctly and with instances. Objective.

Style?
Choices are basically: factual and direct, humorous, mixture of both.

Decision:
Irony and sarcasm, but light-hearted.

Drafting

Our article is to be on university students. Suppose you have read the evidence of a study showing that students on degree courses spend practically no money on books and spend little time reading widely in their subject. They simply read the minimal amount necessary to pass.

First draft: Your task is to write a 400-word article, using sarcasm/irony but including factual reference, on this topic, for an outlet in a national daily newspaper ('quality').

example:
Hitch-Hike to the Reading Festival

Yes, it's that time of year again - the autumn, and the first semester of the new academic year. They'll all be clamouring around the motorway-sliproads, thumbing their way to the Reading Festival. Our young people, our hope for the future, about to sit around on hot lawns, sipping lager and reading, reading, reading... until they are dizzy or want to barf over a fence, sick on words.

But I know that most of them will take the wrong car, travel to the wrong campus. In fact, John Smith's research at Keele shows that 79% of them will never get to Reading at all. No, they will consume an average of eight and a half books in their first semester. That's three months by the way.

I'll still hang about, flapping my bright green reading-list in case any do come my way. I'll flap it around in a classroom maybe, as they wait for enlightenment. Apparently, your average student expects knowledge to enter into the body by osmosis, leaving out the printed word entirely. It all happens on the slip-roads, they say. Or are they slip-up roads, leading to the unemployment office, where less interesting reading awaits them?

This is your first draft. It needs three things changing or developing.

1. More reference to facts/ events

2. Clearer application to ideas on why reading is important

3. The reasons why reading is declining.

But the important point is that you have a draft. The editing process will simply involve changes such as this one:

I'll flap around in the classroom ,maybe, as they wait for enlightenment- becoming more ironic:

I'll lecture them to shame them, quoting what they should have read as I flap......

Try an article now, on any topic within your area, and then edit to a longer or shorter length, changing to keep the angle you need.

Submission

If we then submitted the article, for a specified slot in the publication, we would need to write a covering letter responding to a particular writing task:

'Dear Editor,
Iam a freelance writer specialising in educational topics, and I
am responding to your call for contributions to the
'Megaphone' column with a short article on the crisis in
undergraduate reading -or lack of it. My published work is
summarised on the attached sheet.

You would then add the usual brief details about why you
wrote it, your relevant experience etc.

Log the feedback

As mentioned in Chapter Two, the important point is the
follow-up to all submissions. Log the responses to the article
from the editor. You might use this method, in case you are
too busy to do re-writing immediately:

writing response task pending date
Good, but short add paragraph need ref. to research   11/3

This has been a brief example of a typical submission to a
newspaper or magazine Notice that, to some writing freelance
factual/instructional articles, this would be one of several being
processed through editing, re-writing for new markets and so
on. Overall organisation is the key to success.

This last chapter has been a focus on the actual application of
writing to a typical market. The three stages of *research-*
writing- logging have been used.

Follow the advice here about careful planning, being sure of your interests and abilities, and maintain a serious, professional attitude at all times, and your chances of success in writing will be maximised. Good luck with your freelancing, and never overlook the value of self-assessment and concentration on what you as an individual are best suited to producing.

Now read the KEY POINTS from Chapter Ten

KEY POINTS FROM CHAPTER TEN
A SUMMARY AND AN INITIAL EXERCISE

- Find a specific 'slot' or opening and study the features and conventions required.

- Study the style and treatment. Assess the identity of the piece as a regular in the publication.

- Write a first draft, then edit according to a model in the publication.

- Submit, with an explanation of your rationale. Log the feedback -always.

11

MULTI-SKILLS REQUIRED

The world of the freelance writer has changed rapidly over the last few decades, mainly as there have been revolutions in both the periodical industry and in publishing.

As most freelance writing depends on building relationships with publishers, editors and contacts of all kinds in the writer's specialist areas, then some sense of stability is important. Most writers will complain that one of the most persistent obstacles in the way of success is the nature of editing. Editors will change all the time, either as internal shuffling of personnel takes place or as staff move to other companies. What often happens is that a writer will have an article accepted, and the editor will say that he or she is happy to see more of the writer's work, then perhaps a few more pieces will attract some interest. The rapport is there, and then the editor moves and the whole process has to begin again.

Our best tool to use in order to work against this, or at least to play down the negative effects of such frustrating experience, is to consider the nature of the skills involved in writing for a market. The foundation of that is made by thinking about organising yourself with the right resources and materials. Success in that depends on gathering resources for a wide market, having subjects, themes and contacts ready for the new opportunity when it comes.

A Case Study of My Own

My own writing career exemplifies the operation of this adaptation and need for planning. I began as a poet and an academic writer. My publications tended to be author-studies, poems in magazines or booklets, and occasional articles. Then I began to accept that what was deep in me was a love of history, and that I had put other things before that. This was the process that happened, and it should provide a template for the kind of experience you may well have as you progress:

Phase One

A recognition that there is an expanding interest in your subject – in print or other media.

Example: The shelves in newsagents had more and more publications on all kinds of history, many of these as a result of a boom in researching family history and genealogy.

Phase Two

Questions about what particular version of historical writing could I produce?

Example: There is a whole spectrum of styles, outlets and readership groups. For instance, I would say that the range of magazines, journals and books goes from academic monographs to features on such topics as 'My Dad was a Spy' for a popular magazine.

Phase Three

A selection of my own area and range, which has been crime and law in history.

Example: Once that was decided, these obvious categories emerged:

Case histories
Biographies of significant people
Police subjects
Famous/infamous murders
Specific crimes and social change, e.g. suicide (a crime until 1961).

This then began to open out as I learned more about the social and legal history behind subjects.

Phase Four
Now I was more certain of the potential of the range I had, so I gathered materials and sources for writing.

This broke down into these categories:
Library book resources
Newspapers and journals on microfilm
Memoirs of professionals
Actual primary sources such as legal documents in archives, interviews with people/ letters and unpublished experience

I became, gradually, a crime writer and crime historian. What I had to do to attain that position is a pattern for all freelance work. This is because what tends to happen is that the area and range you think you have determined tends to open out as you learn more about the market. For instance, one article on a specific murder case could have these outlets:

1. A crime magazine
2. A more serious history publication: the murder may have arisen because of a specific social, economic or political subject.

3. A popular publication such as a family history magazine.

Point 2 may be illustrated by a case I researched in Bradford in the mid-nineteenth century. A marching band from an Orange Lodge was attacked by a gang and a man was killed. What provoked the attack was the playing of a particular rebel song on a period of Irish history that was divisive socially and ideologically. To write that case I had to explore the resonance of that song, as well as investigate the nature of the Irish population in Bradford at that time.

In doing that research, I found myself having to use standard reference books, the internet and publications on musical history. Therefore what has happened to me as a writer over the last five years is that I have gathered a whole cluster of ancillary skills, all backing up my writing. This would be a checklist of what I have learned, and all of these have deepened my writing style and also the narrative texture in the writing:

Finding and sifting materials
Comparing varying testimonies to events
Reading a range of writing in different publications (sometimes in foreign languages)
Using local archives
Interviewing people and writing to them
Taking photographs to use with articles

Underpinning all this has been a gradual understanding of what kinds of historical writing match specific outlets.

What are the Skills?

In practical terms, the skills we need more and more today involve more than the creative writing itself. These are the steps in the normal process of writing a non-fiction book for instance:

1.   The writer studies the market and the publishers

2.   The writer approaches the publisher with the idea for a book (a letter of enquiry only)

3.   If there is an encouraging response, a synopsis and sample writing has to be delivered

4.   If that leads to a contract, the writer then has to agree to a deadline, length, additional features more than the bare text, and of course all the legal topics.

5.   The writer writes the book

6.   The editor or editors work on that and the writer adapts

7.   The blurb has to be written – often by the writer

8.   The proofs will arrive for the writer to work on.

9.   The cover will be agreed on.

10. The book is marketed.

What I have missed out there is the often formidable document called an Author Questionnaire, common for non-fiction books. This is a solid document asking the writer for all kinds of information which will help the marketing of the book. This will ask for contacts, publications, professional societies, significant anniversaries, potential places for review, a description of the book and some biographical information. Often it will ask for full contact information of editors, publications and companies who might be useful to the book.

The skills backing up the actual writing then, fall into three categories:
Pre-writing
Complementary to the writing
Post-writing

 In the pre-writing the elements are mostly around the effort to find a subject that has a niche in the market – a current need. Typical of this is a biography, as that may involve the aim to produce a life of someone whose story has not been told for several decades. Or it might be an offer to write a volume in a series such as 'Great Welsh Writers.' Complementary to the writing are all the information-gathering activities. Then post-writing involves the marketing involvement.

Complementary to the Writing: A scenario

Returning to my crime writing as an example, this scenario illustrates the organisation and resources I have gradually adopted and acquired:

1   The chapter or article is on a Victorian murder.

2   I make sure I have these resources to hand: reference works, newspaper cuttings, internet sources, photocopies of secondary sources in a file and any primary sources I might have.

3   As I write, I turn to these when needed.

4   The texture and vocabulary, with the range of reference then is enriched, so that, for example, in the course of writing one of my books, *Lincolnshire Murders*, in one chapter I needed this factual back-up:

Details of a specific poison
Legal information about adversarial procedure in court
Local geography
Accounts of a particular person's drinking habits
Research on the defences normally raised in court at the time

In some freelance writing on crime and law I have even had to check on regional dialect and on the internal design of public houses. All freelance writing opens out, all the time, into areas of related knowledge. This is of course both a pleasure and a handicap. The writer in this context has to know and want that feeling of deep satisfaction that comes from collating a mass of information, editing and selecting what is used and what is not used, and then crafting everything into a readable piece for a designated market.

The Reference Resources

My own library for writing on crime and law consists of these categories.

Reference Books: mainly dictionaries of law and history. But also works on anatomy, language, architecture, geography and police organisation are useful. What tends to happen is that the 'jigsaw effect' happens in writing. You place one piece of information into the writing, from a good source, and then a word has to be checked, often in several places. For instance, I once wrote an article based on a case in a village I had assumed was in Yorkshire (from my established knowledge) but only when the article was written did I realise that two sources had differed and one source had the place, correctly, in Nottinghamshire.

Then we have the specialist societies, journals and web sites: these vary in usefulness and you have to select carefully. But there is one great virtue in having access to specialist knowledge, and that is your acquisition of rather obscure and reliable information that will enrich the writing. One society I have joined has a e-mail list (confidential and for members only) so that I can ask for information directly, 'to the horse's mouth' as it were.

Archives available on line are invaluable, and every area of work has it own group of these. Clearly, newspaper archives such as *The Times* are of especially high regard. But there are also other very useful resources, such as the 'Athens' system of accessing journals in all areas, on-line, with a password and subscription.

Finally, the subject of networking has to emerge once again. In that context, the local Arts Council organisations and other professional groups are of real importance, as they generally issue directories of writers and artists in particular areas. All these resources come together and integrate in your writing; there is factual basis to all freelance writing, of course, and that, in the end, will be the ultimate criterion on which your piece is judged. With a few exceptions, freelance writing does not really consist of material 'dashed off' for a deadline, although that myth seems to persist. On the contrary, it is a life of hard labour and professionalism, with a massive sense of satisfaction when the finished piece is exactly what the writer aimed at when there was just an idea and an outline in the head and not even on paper.

NOW READ THE KEY POINTS FROM CHAPTER ELEVEN

KEY POINTS FROM CHAPTER ELEVEN
MULTI-SKILLS REQUIRED

- Take time to research and understand the changing markets in your area

- Research the sources well

- Understand and develop your own range of skills

- Be prepared to learn from experience

- Cultivate professional societies and contacts

- Use a workable personal resource centre.

Bibliographical Resource
Section

12

BIBLIOGRAPHY AND RESOURCES

These are some of the main publications and resources you will need to establish yourself as a freelance writer. We all have our personal tastes of course, as in choosing which style guide to use and rely on or which dictionary to consult, but these resources are ones which have been used – often widely use – and have been recommended. Most are texts I have used myself over the years.

Often, some of the most useful books for the freelance writer are to be found in the area of media studies and in the professional trade publications, so I have included some of the magazines related to that context.

Books

<u>General</u>
Bell, Julia and Magrs, Paul, *The Creative Writing Coursebook* (Macmillan) 2001

Bolton, Gillie *The Therapeutic Potential of Creative Writing* (Jessica Kingsley) 2000

Browne, Renni and King, Dave, *Self-Editing for Fiction Writers* (HarperCollins) 1993

Ferris, Stewart *How to get Published* (Summersdale) 2005

Goldberg, Natalie, *Writing Down the Bones* (Shambala) 1986

Klauser, Henriette Anne, *Write it Down, Make it Happen* (Simon and Shuster) 2001

Mills, Paul, *Writing in Action* (Routledge) 1996

Ruthven, Suzanne, *Creative Pathways* (Ignotus Press) 2002

Sellers, Susan, T*aking Reality by Surprise* (Women's Press) 1991

Sweeney, Matthew and Williams, John Hartley, *Writing Poetry* (Hodder) 1997

Walker, Kate, *Writing Romantic Fiction* (Straightforward) 2002

Whale, John, *Put it in Writing* (Orion) 1999

White, Ted, Broadcast News Reporting and Producing, (Focal; Press) 2005
Reference

The Writers and Artists' Yearbook (annual) A&C Black

Turner, Barry, The Writer's Handbook   (annual) Macmillan

The Small Press Guide   (annual) from Writer's Bookshop

The Guide to Book Publishers (annual) from Writer's Bookshop

McCallum, Chris, and Wells, Gordon, The Magazine Writer's Handbook Writer's Bookshop

<u>Magazines</u>

The Bookseller,
Endeavour House, 5th floor,
189, Shaftesbury Avenue,
London,
WC2H 8TJ

Freelance Market News,
Sevendale House,
7, Dale Street,
Manchester
M1 1JB

Myslexia,
P.O.Box 656
Newcastle upon Tyne
NE99 1PZ

Press Gazette,
John Carpenter House
John Carpenter Street
London EC4Y OAN

Writing magazine,
Fifth Floor,
31-32 Park Row
Leeds LS51 5JD

Writers' Forum,
P.O.Box 3229
Bournemouth BH1 IZS

Organisations

Arvon Foundation,
Totleigh barton,
Sheepwash, Beaworthy,
Devon EX21 5NS

National Poetry Foundation,
27, Mill Road,
Fareham,
Hampshire PO16 OTH

National Association of Writers in Education
P.O.Box 1
Sheriff Hutton,
York YO 60 7YU

National Association of Writers Groups
The Arts Cenbtre
Biddick Lane,
Washington, NE38 2AB

National Union of Journalists,
Headland House,
308, Gray's Inn Road,
London WC1X 8DP

Picture research Association,
10 Marrick House
Mortimer Crescent
London NW6 5NY

The Publishers Association,
29B Montague Street
London WC1B 5BW

The Society of Authors,
84, Drayton Gardens,
London SW10 9SB

Society of Women Writers and Journalists,
14 Laburnum Walk
Rustington
Littlehampton BN16 3QW

****

www.straightforwardco.co.uk

All titles, listed below, in the Straightforward Guides Series can be purchased online, using credit card or other forms of payment by going to www.straightfowardco.co.uk A discount of 25% per title is offered with online purchases.

Law

A Straightforward Guide to:
Consumer Rights
Bankruptcy Insolvency and the Law
Employment Law
Private Tenants Rights
Family law
Small Claims in the County Court
Contract law
Intellectual Property and the law
Divorce and the law
Leaseholders Rights
The Process of Conveyancing
Knowing Your Rights and Using the Courts
Producing Your own Will
Housing Rights
The Bailiff the law and You
Probate and The Law
Company law
What to Expect When You Go to Court
Guide to Competition Law
Give me Your Money-Guide to Effective Debt Collection
Caring for a Disabled Child

General titles

Letting Property for Profit
Buying, Selling and Renting property
Buying a Home in England and France
Bookkeeping and Accounts for Small Business

Creative Writing
Freelance Writing
Writing Your own Life Story
Writing performance Poetry
Writing Romantic Fiction
Speech Writing

Teaching Your Child to Read and write
Teaching Your Child to Swim
Raising a Child-The Early Years

Creating a Successful Commercial Website
The Straightforward Business Plan
The Straightforward C.V.
Successful Public Speaking

Handling Bereavement
Play the Game-A Compendium of Rules
Individual and Personal Finance
Understanding Mental Illness
The Two-Minute Message
Tiling for Beginners

Go to: www.straightforwardco.co.uk

Straightforward Publishing

If you have any queries concerning this publication or would like to write for us, contact us at:

info@straightforwardco.co.uk

Companion titles in the creative writing series.

A Straightforward Guide to Creative Writing
ISBN 9781847161932

Writing Romantic Fiction
ISBN 9781847161925

Writing Performance Poetry
ISBN 9781847161918

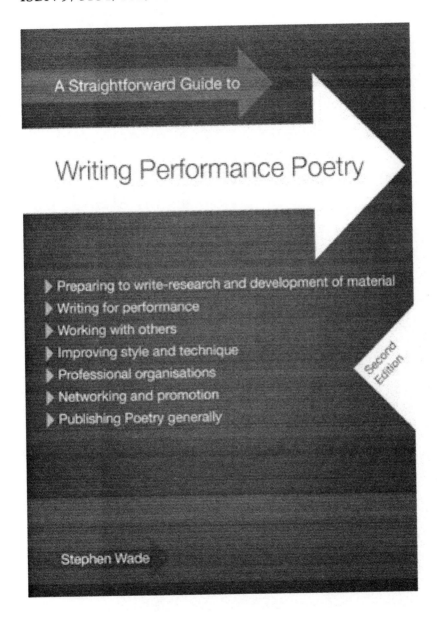

A Straightforward Guide to

Writing Performance Poetry

▶ Preparing to write-research and development of material
▶ Writing for performance
▶ Working with others
▶ Improving style and technique
▶ Professional organisations
▶ Networking and promotion
▶ Publishing Poetry generally

Second Edition

Stephen Wade